PRELUDE TO BRUISE

PRELUDE
TO
BRUISE

POETRY

SAEED JONES

COFFEE HOUSE PRESS
MINNEAPOLIS
2014

Coffee House Press books are available to the trade through our primary distributor, Consortium Book Sales & Distribution, cbsd.com. For personal orders, catalogs, or other information, write to: info@coffeehousepress.org.

Coffee House Press is a nonprofit literary publishing house. Support from private foundations, corporate giving programs, government programs, and generous individuals helps make the publication of our books possible. We gratefully acknowledge their support in detail in the back of this book.

Visit us at coffeehousepress.org.

LIBRARY OF CONGRESS CATALOGING-IN-PUBLICATION DATA

Jones, Saeed.
[Poems. Selections]
Prelude to bruise / by Saeed Jones.
pages cm
ISBN 978-1-56689-374-9 (pbk.)
ISBN 978-1-56689-384-8 (ebook)
I. Title.
PS3610.O6279P74 2014
811'.6—dc23
2014008086

PRINTED IN THE UNITED STATES

For my mother
Nam-myoho-renge-kyo

The man in ecstasy and the man drowning—
both throw up their arms.

—KAFKA

ANTHRACITE

A voice mistook for stone,
jagged black fist

thrown miles through space, through
doors of dark matter.

Heard you crack open the field's skull
where you landed.

Halo of smoke ruined the sky
and you were a body now

naked and bruised in the cratered cotton.
Could have been a meteorite

except for those strip-mined eyes, each
a point of fossilized night.

Bringing water and a blanket,
I asked, "Which of your lives is this,

third or fifth?" Your answer, blues
a breeze to soak my clothes

in tears. With my palm pressed
to your lips, hush. When they hear

you, they will want you. Beware
of how they want you;

in this town everything born black
also burns.

1

INSOMNIAC

Small with wild legs, the boy stole your eyes
the day he was born.

In a language you've tried to keep
from him, your name is *mother of sorrows*.

When he does not answer your latest call, dream
him grown and gone: far off, a vial of your tears
on his nightstand.

In the autumn of his blood, he will siphon your hurt
to a child dying of thirst; the only inheritance
of worth in the village of your synapses.

But—for now—he's still your boy. Sweet little
wreck. Check the room you've locked him in.

CLOSET OF RED

In place of *no*, my leaking mouth spills foxgloves.
Trumpets of tongued blossoms litter the locked closet.
Up to my ankles in petals, the hanged gowns close in,
mother multiplied, more—there're always more
corseted ghosts, red-silk bodies crowd
my mouth. I would say *no, please*;
I would say *sorry, Papa*; I would never
ask for mother again, but dresses dressed
in dresses are dresses that own this garnet dark,
this mouth. These hands can't find
the walls, only more mothers
emptied out.

THE BLUE DRESS

Her blue dress is a silk train is a river
is water seeps into the cobblestone streets of my sleep, is still
    raining
is monsoon brocade, is winter stars stitched into puddles
is good-bye in a flooded, antique room, is good-bye in a room of
    crystal bowls
and crystal cups, is the ring-ting-ring of water dripping from the
    mouths
of crystal bowls and crystal cups, is the Mississippi River is a
    hallway, is leaks
like tears from windowsills of a drowned house, is windows
    open to waterfalls
is a bed is a small boat is a ship, is a current come to carry me in
    its arms
through the streets, is me floating in her dress through the
    streets
is only the moon sees me floating through the streets, is me in a
    blue dress
out to sea, is my mother is a moon out to sea.

ISAAC, AFTER MOUNT MORIAH

Asleep on the roof when rain comes,
water collects in the dips of his collarbone.

Dirty-haired boy, my rascal, my sacrifice. Never
an easy dream. I watch him wrestle my shadow, eyelids
trembling, one fist ready for me.

Leave him a blanket, leave him alone.

Night before, found him caked in dirt,
sleeping in a ditch; wet black stones for pillows.

What kind of father does he make me, this boy
I find tangled in the hair of willows, curled fetal
in the grove?

Once, I found him in a far field, the mountain's peak
like a blade above us both.

PRETENDING TO DROWN

The only regret is that I waited
longer than a breath
to scatter the sun's reflection
with my body.

New stars burst upon the water
when you pulled me in.

On the shore, our clothes
begged us to be good boys again.

Every stick our feet touched
a snapping turtle, every shadow
a water moccasin.

Excuses to swim closer to one another.

I sank into the depths to see you
as the lake saw you: cut in half
by the surface, taut legs kicking,
the rest of you sky.

Suddenly still, a clear view
of what you knew I wanted
to see.

When I resurfaced, slick grin,
knowing glance; you pushed me
back under.

I pretended to drown,
then swallowed you whole.

BOY IN A STOLEN EVENING GOWN

In this field of thistle, I am the improbable
lady. How I wear the word: sequined weight
snagging my saunter into overgrown grass, blonde
split-end blades. I waltz in an acre of bad wigs.

Sir who is no one, sir who is yet to come, I need you
to undo this zipped back, trace the chiffon
body I've borrowed. See how I switch my hips

for you, dry grass cracking under my pretend
high heels? Call me and I'm at your side,
one wildflower behind my ear. Ask me
and I'll slip out of this softness, the dress

a black cloud at my feet. I could be the boy
wearing nothing, a negligee of gnats.

BOY AT EDGE OF WOODS

After his gasp and *god damn*,
after his zipper closes
its teeth, his tongue leaves
its shadows, leaves me
alone to pick pine needles
from my hair, to brush brown
leaves off my shirt as blades
of light hang from the trees,
as I relearn my legs, mud-
stained knees, and walk back
to my burning house.

TERRIBLE BOY

In the field, one paw of the lion-clawed bathtub
glints in the light. Lukewarm buckets of water
carried for miles. And I will pay brightly

for this slick body. Unclean under
a back-turned sun, I sing the sins
that brought me here:

> I turned the family portrait facedown
> when he was on me,

> fed gasoline to the roots of forsythia,

> broke a mirror to slim
> my reflection's waist,

> what he calls me is not my name

and I love it. Damask chair
beside the tub and on it, handmade armor
of bone.

Out of the water, in a wet-wheat towel
I wake
in my unlit room.

Father standing at the door.

DAEDALUS, AFTER ICARUS

Boys begin to gather around the man like seagulls.
He ignores them entirely, but they follow him
from one end of the beach to the other.
Their footprints burn holes in the sand.
It's quite a sight, a strange parade:
a man with a pair of wings strapped to his arms
followed by a flock of rowdy boys.
Some squawk and flap their bony limbs.
Others try to leap now and then, stumbling
as the sand tugs at their feet. One boy pretends to fly
in a circle around the man, cawing in his face.

We don't know his name or why he walks
along our beach, talking to the wind.
To say nothing of those wings. A woman yells
to her son, *Ask him if he'll make me a pair.*
Maybe I'll finally leave your father.
He answers our cackles with a sudden stop,
turns, and runs toward the water.
The children jump into the waves after him.
Over the sounds of their thrashes and giggles,
we hear a boy say, *We don't want wings.*
We want to be fish now.

BOY IN A WHALEBONE CORSET

The acre of grass is a sleeping
swarm of locusts, and in the house
beside it, tears too are mistaken.
Thin streams of kerosene
when night throws itself against
the wall, when Nina Simone sings
in the next room without her body
and I'm against the wall, bruised
but out of mine: dream-headed
with my corset still on, stays
slightly less tight, bones against
bones, broken glass on the floor,
dance steps for a waltz
with no partner. Father in my room
looking for more *sissy clothes*
to burn. Something pink in his fist,
negligee, lace, fishnet, whore.
His son's a whore this last night
of Sodom. And the record skips
and skips and skips. Corset still on,
nothing else, I'm at the window;
he's in the field, gasoline jug,
hand full of matches, night made
of locusts, column of smoke
mistaken for Old Testament God.

BOY FOUND INSIDE A WOLF

Red is at the end of black. Pitch-black unthreads
and swings garnet

in what I thought was home. I'm climbing
out of my father. His love a wet shine

all over me. He knew I would come
to this: one small fist

punching a hole
to daylight.

BOY AT THRESHOLD

The front door kicked open
to a sky of windblown herons, pewter
wings bent back

by dark gust. If I were your blood,
I would fear this feathered dusk,
but I've always wanted to be dangerous.

The air grabs my lapel, rough-tongued
gale, and drags me free.

AFTER THE FIRST SHOT

I run the dark winter
coatless and a shirt of briar,

season of black sycamore
thickets, then the startle

of open fields. Bare feet
cracking earth. Each mile

birthing three more.
There are sorrel horses

herding inside me.
In a four-legged night,

clouds sink into the trees,
refuse me morning

and mourning, but I pass
what I thought was the end

of myself. To answer
your rifle's last question:

if you ever find me,
I won't be there.

LAST CALL

Night presses the gunmetal O of its mouth
against my own; I can't help how I answer.

He is the taste of smoke, mesquite-laced tip
of the tongue. Silhouetted, a body always

pulling away, but his shirt collar in my fists,
I pull him back. Need another double-black

kiss. I've got more hunger than my body can hold.
Bloated with want, I'm the man who waits

for the moon to drown before I let the lake
grab my ankles & take me into its muddy mouth.

They say a city is at the bottom of all that water.
Oh, marauder. Make me a drink. I'm on my way.

2

"DON'T LET THE SUN SET ON YOU"

In 1990
     you're in Kentucky
     on Highway 461

Thank God, it's not dark   yet.

Just enough light

for you   to see

     the sign.

          Off the right-of-way
          hillside, almost overgrown

NIGGER, DON'T LET THE SUN SET ON YOU

     hillside, almost overgrown

sundown, 6 p.m.

     YOU BETTER RUN

IF YOU CAN READ

     THIS SIGN

     hillside, Highway 461

Even if you can't read
         this sign, you know

darkness, don't you?

PRELUDE TO BRUISE

In Birmingham, said the burly man—

Boy, be
a bootblack.

Your back, blue-black.
Your body,   burning.

      I like my black boys broke, or broken.
      I like to break my black boys in.

See this burnished
brown leather belt?
You see it, boy?

      Are you broke, or broken?
        I'm gonna break your back in.

Good boy. Begin: bend
over my boot,

      (or I'll bend you over my lap—*rap rap*)

again, bend. Better,

butt out, tongue out,
lean in.

     Now, spit-shine.
     Spit-polish.

     My boot, black.
     Your back, blue-black.

Good boy.
Black boy, blue-black boy.
Bad boy—*rap rap*.

You've been broken in.
Begin again, bend.

COYOTE CRY

Listen to my darkness, my half-eclipsed notes.
Mistake them for the sound of a lonely woman
wailing as she roams the hills. She needs you
like I need you. Ignore the warnings;
hurry to me. Why aren't you here yet?
Can't you hear her trouble? Cold air
dries her muddy footprints to a path
of hard, open mouths. If she retraces her steps,
the footprints will eat her. Oh, farmer.
Ragged pines snatch her cries and keep them.
That's why I cry. Hurry, little one.
Climb the broken stone stairs into the hills.
Climb them into the night's throat.

JASPER, 1998

in memory of James Byrd Jr.

I.

Go back: my throat still
    crowded with dirt
                and loose teeth
but I speak
    (tongue slick with iron)
but I speak
in the language of sharp turns.

II.

Go back: I accept this ride.

Tired, don't want to walk
        home.
It's not far, but far
        enough. I accept
this ride.
        Three nice men,
white men,
        a bit too nice,
but I accept: no backseat driver.

        Smile, ride, quiet.

Could have taken
        that last turn,
but I accept these men,
        their sense of direction,
but I live
        on the other side of town.

Smile, ride, quiet.

Another turn
        I wouldn't take. This road,
back road,
wrong way,
too far.

Smile
> with questions
> in my eyes.

Ride
> backseat, sure is
> better than walking.

Quiet
> middle of nowhere,
> tight-lipped white men,

> no other cars around,
> no sound but my heart.

Where (say it)
Where (louder)
Where
are we going?

III.

Chain gang, work song, back road,
my body.
Chain gang, work song, back road,
my body.
These men play me dirty
            tell my back to sing or break.
Hard-won rattle
      of chains
            dragged behind this truck,
louder than what little sound
      is left in my throat.

Pavement becomes a skin-tight
drum,
            they take my teeth
            for piano keys.
My God,
this song: one man
                  chain gang, playing this road.
            Every stick,
            every pebble: this road
                        this song.

Hear me, Jasper.
Hear me for miles.

LOWER NINTH

New Orleans, March 2011

For the city and its clogged arteries of light,
a ward of wild grass to answer the absence
of foundation. How the jasmine vine rests
its hands on the abandoned sill for a month,
then pulls itself into the cool dark. And how,
driving through (but not walking), you point
to where you once were sent for milk, detergent,
whatever was needed from the corner store
and the jagged slab of concrete the water left
behind. You wonder which states the neighbors
moved to, and if they are thinking of what you
see: how the crabgrass eventually won, streets
empty aside from the refrigerator that floated
into the avenue unquestioned and stayed,
and how low it all is and why.

DRAG

The dress is an oil slick. The dress
ruins everything. In a hotel room
by the water, I put it on when
he says, *I want to watch you take it off.*
Zipping me up, he kisses the mile
markers of my spine. I can't afford
this view. From here, I see a city
that doesn't know it's already
drowning. My neck shivers from
the trail of his tongue. I keep my
eyes on the window, just past
his bald spot. He's short. I can see
the rain that has owned us for weeks
already. The dress will survive us.
The dress will be here when men
come in boats to survey the damage.
He makes me another drink, puts
on some jazz, and the dress begins
to move without me. Slow like some-
thing that knows it cannot be stopped,
the dress seeps. The dress slides
with my body floating inside,
an animal caught in the sludge.
If he wraps his arms around me,
it will be the rest of his life.
I don't even know what I am
in this dress; I just sway with
my arms open and wait.

KUDZU

I won't be forgiven
for what I've made
of myself.
Soil recoils
from my hooked kisses.
Pines turn their backs
on me. They know
what I can do
with the wrap of my legs.
Each summer,
when the air becomes crowded
with want, I set all my tongues
upon you.
To quiet this body,
you must answer
my tendriled craving.
All I've ever wanted
was to kiss crevices, pry them open,
and flourish within dew-slick
hollows.
How you mistake
my affection.
If I ever strangled sparrows,
it was only because I dreamed
of better songs.

BEHEADED KINGDOM

I.

With his one good knife, a door is cut to where the spine waits: patient,
then flaring. All my lights turned on. A scream is loosed,
grey silk sound pulled out by hooks, black before the filaments.
Quiet, he begs, rakish doctor. Then a hand goes in.

II.

He takes his time to walk the bright house of me.
Each room rococo, floored with mahogany. A wealth of blood cells flickering
red, then blue, red, then blue in shadow boxes. Here, a room of rare orchids
the color of a drinker's liver.

III.

Do you understand the song you've sent walking through my catacombs
of marrow? Black parasol notes hum, dirge of the removed
lung. I now know the promise of a body scooped hollow, tea lights
in the torso's cave. You've come inside from another country
and I have so much to give.

THRALLDOM

I survived on mouthfuls of hyacinth.
My hunger did not apologize.

Stamens licked clean, pollinated
throat; Beauty was what I choked on.

When the men with cruel tongues
worked me, each grunt gnashed

between my teeth. One fogged
night to the next, my palm

pressed against each thrust.
How else to say *more*

please under the sweat
and heave of their bodies?

CRUEL BODY

You answer his fist   and the blow
shatters you to sparks.

Unconscious   is a better place, but swim back
to yourself.

Behind a door you can't open,   he drinks
to keep loving you,

then wades out into the blue hour.

Still on the floor, waiting   for your name
to claim your mouth.

     Get up. Find your legs,
leave.

THALLIUM

If I held out the candle, paraffin burning for him,
then swallowed all the light, if

in the dark, I was a cobra's tongue,
        how could it have been his fault?

Robber baron, unzipped vagabond, he mistook me
for the comfort of a small creek, water crawling along the backs
of rocks, emerald house beside it,

me at the door in nothing
but welcome.

Over wine, I warned him
soft

you can't sleep here; you won't
wake up.

In the snuffed room, my touch   serrated
bit of tooth

or switchblade.

Even a peacock feather comes to a point.

He thought
I was kissing him.

HE THINKS HE CAN LEAVE ME

by leaving me,
       but even now

I walk
burning

          through the empty streets
          of his mind.

Lonely
little town, no sound

          but my footsteps.

I grin,
mouthful of hell

        my teeth
        soot black.

In curlicues of smoke, I sing
his name
         to the night

and his darkness
mistakes me

         for sunrise.

3

SECONDHAND (SMOKE)

I borrowed his body just like
this.   I wanted, so I had his wrist
like this: held the bones easiest to break   like so,
   arched in question
and the cigarette,   a sixth finger lit, tilted,   ash outlining the
   exhaled *yes*—

    Even if the *yes* was palimpsest,
each breath confusing the other for a blow of smoke,
    it matters that I had him here   once.
Even held down, even pinned, ersatz: the idea of his body,
a *yes* of my own.

    I stole his tongue; now he can't say *no*.
His *yes* is mine to keep,   mine to answer
my own questions with, like:
    Now that I've mined you, are you mine?

    I spell his body with smoke,   breathe him
into the seat beside me. Black lung to blacker lung
and ever waiting: his answer is   just   like—

BODY & KENTUCKY BOURBON

In the dark, my mind's night, I go back
to your work-calloused hands, your body

and the memory of fields I no longer see.
Cheek wad of chew tobacco,

Skoal-tin ring in the back pocket
of threadbare jeans, knees

worn through entirely. How to name you:
farmhand, Kentucky boy, lover.

The one who taught me to bear
the back-throat burn of bourbon.

Straight, no chaser, a joke in our bed,
but I stopped laughing; all those empty bottles,

kitchen counters covered with beer cans
and broken glasses. To realize you drank

so you could face me the morning after,
the only way to choke down rage at the body

sleeping beside you. What did I know
of your father's backhand or the pine casket

he threatened to put you in? Only now,
miles and years away, do I wince at the jokes:

white trash, farmer's tan, good ole boy.
And now, alone, I see your face

at the bottom of my shot glass
before my own comes through.

ECLIPSE OF MY THIRD LIFE

Hunger is who we are
under a black lacquered moon.

Undone in his flashlit arms, is this my body anymore?

Red Chinese kite in the night of my throat,
no one can see.

Unpaved road that veers
into fragments of bone, a drive only he knows.

Spine stitched to shadow's edge, I lose my head
to grass when his want walks

the length of me, king of my beheaded kingdom.

Stars are just jewelry stolen from graves, he sighs,
pressing me into loam, amaryllis shoots

already owning my dark. I'll wake, a garden
gated in April light,

my veins in every leaf.

GUILT

Five years gone but my body
is back in the truck beside you,

speeding toward the dogs
we cannot see but are about to hit.

It is not dark. Midday, windows
down. Wind runs all its hands

through the hair of every tree
we pass & maybe this is where

I close my eyes & say, "It sounds
like the ocean." Maybe you are

on the edge of an answer when
three dogs that were not in the road

suddenly are. Before I can see
their eyes, before I am even sure

they are there, the yelp of injury
& smack against metal are the same

sound. You pull over. I open my
door before you can say you

are too afraid to get out. The walk
to the front of your truck is hours,

but I am there now & the dog
is not. No dent. No blood.

The road that was an empty road
is an empty road. The wind

& trees have turned into waves again.
You don't believe me. "We hit

that dog," you hiss, now out
of the truck. We both stare

at the dent, the blood; the dogs
are not there. A rustle

in the trees at the edge of the road,
but no eyes looking out at us.

SLEEPING ARRANGEMENT

I've decided: you will stay
under our bed, on the floor

not even in the space between
mattress and metal frame.

Take your hand out
from under my pillow.

And take your sheets with you.
Drag them under. Make pretend ghosts.

I can't have you rattling the bedsprings
so keep still, keep quiet.

Mistake yourself for shadows.
Learn the lullabies of lint.

*

I will do right by you:
crumbs brushed off my sheets,

white chocolate chips
or the corners of crackers.

Count on the occasional dropped grape,
a peach pit with dried yellow hairs.

I've heard some men can survive
on dust mites alone for weeks at a time.

There's a magnifying glass on the nightstand,
in case it comes to that.

APOLOGIA

If I started with the words *He made me*—
not like *He created me,*

not like *With my clothes off, you can still see his thumbprints*
in the clay that became my skin.

No. If I started with *He made me*
lick the taste of bullet

from the barrel of his revolver
would you use your body to guard my body tonight?

The roof has been ripped off and the stars refuse
to peel their stares from my bruises.

I didn't mean *He*
as in God; I meant *the man I traded you for.*

KETAMINE & COMPANY

Strobe-lit and slick with music,
      I set my hair on fire   so you can find me on the dance floor.

What's the word in Spanish?

      Singed, then smoked   out: I'm your black matador, blood only

makes me readier.   I've traded my lungs for fog machines.
              You won't breathe tonight

without getting high on me.

     I'm burning.   I'm not

burning.   I'm

dancing.   I'm hell.   Guernica on all fours. Horse-mouthed and—

How do you say easy?

    The pill on my tongue catches light like a doomed moon

and we throw our half-drunk drinks to the floor.

      Crunch to the crack to the crack to the—

glass shards in my soles;   my diamond moves.

Using my right nostril

now,   use me,   you can

use me if you want,   I'm easy,   I'm so, so easy.

Say it in Spanish. Yeah. Say easy.

I'm good.

I work the dance floor until   I am the dance floor. Get on me,

baby. You promised you wouldn't let me do this

alone.

Why aren't you on me yet?

THRALLDOM II

Bluegrass, horsewhip, blue moon, bruise.
All fours, steel bit, steel gag, work. Good hurt, *hurts good*, his
    lap, smack.
Fishnets, lips pursed, knife wound—red. First pose, third pose,
    head thrown
back. This way, that way, *shit boy*, slap.

Want more, black moor, unmoored, loosed. Limp wrist, broke
    wrist, rag doll, thrown. Backseat, head down, headlights, off.
    His car, his house, locked room, owned. Break loose, new
    town, fake name, loaned.
Run hard, look back, go back, owned.

Same bit, same gag, third pose, smack.
Horsewhip, *hurts bad*, head thrown, slap.
Head down, *shit boy*, look back, bruise. *Want more*,
fight back, *no more*, unleashed, this way
out.

SKIN LIKE BRICK DUST

In bed, your back curved
to answer the heat of my holding

& Harlem was barely awake below us
when a half-broken building

gave in. First, a few loose bricks,
then decades crashed to the street

just as a bus pulled up. Passengers
choking on dust rushed

to escape the wreck
of someone else's memory.

Two blocks beyond gravity,
I pressed into you, into you and away

from all the breaking. I didn't know
your name, so I kissed one

into your mouth. Told myself
I have a body to hold this morning,

then held my own when you
walked out into the sirens.

KINGDOM OF TRICK, KINGDOM OF DRUG

after Lucie Brock-Broido

I.

I lick the sycamore inked onto his sternum.
Hard, sweet ridge of the chest, valley I send sweat into.
With a pen, I bleed mangled birds onto him: robin,
kestrel, sparrow. Pointed tip of his finger
holding them down, he counts. Lest they fly away,
lest they leave him naked and plain. My head against his chest,
robin, kestrel, sparrow, I say, one for each pill.

II.

In bed, we keep combat boots on, scrape our shins
climbing each other—which is to say: I dream I've dragged a tree
into bed with me. Bark against my back, roots and clumps of dirt
poking out from beneath the sheets like feet. Each hour,
another season. It pushes cherry blossoms against my closed eyes,
then just as soon burns leaves red like autumn.

III.

Four nights in, I still don't know his name. And each kiss
is the aftertaste of pills, a white cloud on the tongue. He hates
the names I give him: Tantalus, Orestes, Ganymede. *I don't
need a name* he says, sky-high in the shower, the birds leaking
into stains on his stomach. Orange bottle in hand,
I answer *Hyacinth and Vicodin.* I answer *Xanax and Zephyr.*

IV.

Before he leaves, I tell him about a girl running
through a grove. She trips, gets up just in time. *The ground is so unkind*
laughs the god chasing her. But she's calling out now.
You won't have me. Like it's already over, like she knows.
She stands her ground and leaves weave into her hair. Her skin tans,
then cracks open into bark. And in the branches
of her raised arms, birds.

BLUE PRELUDE

Last night, the ceiling above me ached
with dance. Music dripped down the walls

like rain in an old house. My eyes followed
the couple's steps from one corner

to the other, pictured the press of two chests
against soft breathing, bodies slipping

in and out of candlelight. The hurt
was exquisite. In my empty bed, I dreamed

the record's needle pointed into my back,
spinning me into no one's song.

IN NASHVILLE

At the Silver Saloon, you show me
what a white boy in Wrangler Jeans
can do with my moves. The electric
slide grinds with boot-scootin' boogie.
Two steps to the left, a sunburned woman
outdoes me entirely, throws in some hip
just to call me out. And I feel a bit
betrayed, dancing in this crowd
of snakeskin boots and red, white, and blue
rebel tattoos with the moves I thought
I had some kind of claim to, a way
of mapping out hell with my feet.

4

HIGHWAY 407

Lewisville, TX, August 2011

4 a.m. walks past my wreck
and waiting
      I am done.

Your grief will be useful some day, says no one.

Roadside, my ear still tuned
to asphalt, its moon-crater skin,

I wait.

      The high grass calls you
out of silence.

A vixen,
      apparition

already trotting back:

      oh mother
beastly,

      I stole the planets,
your wet, black eyes.

I lick the dew-damp dirt
           but your feet leave
nothing behind.

I wait

hours into quarters.
          Trucks pass,

white noise trailing radios
like limbs

scattered on the road and I am made
          of waiting.

          My shut eyelids find me

but I know you are not done
with my sleep,

          dead woman.

Behind nothing, I wait.

Leave your feet.
          I lick the dew-damp dirt,
your wet, black eyes.

Oh mother,

already trotting back,

apparition,
        a vixen.

                Out of silence,
the high grass calls you.

I wait,

        roadside, its moon-crater skin,
my ear still tuned to asphalt.

Your grief will be useful some day, says no one.

MERIDIAN

Cinders drift in
    from a fire we can't see.
A breeze
    of sparks, the smell of mesquite
        smoked, crackling.
It could be a family grilling
or another acre
    gone to hell. In this heat,
third week, one hundred degrees
in the shade.
    We're dry tinder.
Water won't answer our questions
anymore; turns to mirage
    when touched.
Forget clothes. Heat knows
    what I want to know: the river
        of sweat through the canyon
        your back becomes
    when my tongue comes
    to cool you. Two men
on fours in this razed field, red clay
to roll in.
    You are my sky burned
to blazing, the dazzle
    before my body's exhausted

collapse, .
    fingers singed,
    breath,
        blue flame.

MERCY

Her ghost slips into the room wearing nothing but the memory
of a song: thin as a note lost in a little girl's throat,

mercy.

If fog had a sound,

if the moon decided to hold its breath,

if she ever heard the way I cry out in my sleep,

mercy.

She knows I'm not well, sees the dark circling my eyes,
one more inheritance,

mercy.

Her stare traces me
and a hand reaches out but Mama, I don't know the words.

MISSISSIPPI DROWNING

I've lined my throat
    with the river bottom's best
    silt,

allowed my fingers to shrivel
    and be taken for crawfish.

    I've laced my eyelashes with algae.

      I blink emerald.
      I blink sea-glass green.

I am whatever gleams
    just under the surface.

Scoop at my sparkle. I'll give you nothing
    but disturbed reflection.

Bring your ear to the water
    and I'll sing you

      down into my arms.

Let me show you how

    to make your lungs
    a home for minnows, how

to let them flicker

like silver

in and out of your mouth
like last words . . .

CASKET SHARP

Your soft cough becomes prognosis. Soon,
cigarette smoke is the inkblot test of lung.

Tell me what you see

and I'll sleepwalk home
to pick out your first and last charcoal suit,

a jade handkerchief for the pocket atop
your excavated chest.

                        I see two men, father & son

but let's not get ahead of ourselves, goner.

And now?

A dirge parades past the empty house,
black silk parasols in hand.

                        I see butterflies of smoke and blood.

And in the aisles of a half-lit church, strangers
walk away from you, whispering, "He looks

good, real sharp." Handsome enough
to bury.

DOMINION

His mouth bleeds when he starts
to sing, but—bless him—he licks

the taste of ruby from his teeth
and sings anyway. Thin blade

of glass lodges in each note,
listen—

he's trying to be better than the rain.

You shut your eyelids to keep him
from slipping into your father's

rumpled body; you stare down
the muddy light locked in the ice

of your drink, but damn if he hasn't
dug up your old man's throat.

THE FABULIST

He puts my hand against his chest
so his nipple can read the lines on my palm.
He insists in his certain voice
that the beat in his chest isn't a beat at all
but an echo: the sound of two fearful feet
heading down into some poorly lit cave
made of bats and blood-red gems.
He tells me again. He's told me before.
The feet walk slower the farther down they go.
No, I say, taking my hand back.
It's a heart. It's always been a heart.
I say it once for him, once for myself.
He steps back and looks at me;
he needs to tell me the story again.

ROOM WITHOUT A GHOST

Sheer, breeze-caught curtains aren't full-bodied,
just billowing. The wind isn't trying

to touch you. Papers rustled, then scattered around the room
mean nothing. Do not read them

in the wind's order. Do not fall to your knees,
deciphering the air and its invisible ink, or look up wide-eyed,

expecting. No one is standing there,
backed against the haze.

Not him. Not *him.*
No one is watching you but you.

DIRGE

With my head half devoured
by fog, I lock myself in your room. Light drums its fingers

against the window, then three bright fingers
finish the dirge on my skin. You are everywhere but where

I need you. Nose pressed to your last pillow, even the memory
    of your breath,
slipping.

        I don't sleep so much as attempt to erase.

When I wake, beside me on the bed is a Ziploc bag from the
    hospital. Inside,
your scissor-shredded clothes, a row of your teeth.

Come back now. Come back
and put your hands over my mouth.

AFTER LAST LIGHT

A moonless night cliff-side steals the sea
from us. What was sapphire beyond churlish blue

is just howl now: waves darker than closed eyelids
wreck the rocks we also can't see. Sunlight forgot

the two of us here. The taste of salt, an ungiven kiss
on our lips. And silence is the rush of blood

in our ears, a violent pause between your question
and what I will not say. I have no answer;

my throat is the ocean now.

HOUR BETWEEN DOG & WOLF

I.

Before the only unbroken mirror, cobalt kimono
undone, embroidered sea at my feet

I'm the self-portrait of my father.

Eyes deep as ravines, night-lined ribcage,
even the rage is his,

this dusk between both of me.

II.

In an hour colored tourmaline, I mistake your guitar
for a body in sleep and smash you into effigy,

splinter your way back into my skin.

My silk-wrapped fists shadowbox your incessant reflection
and break myself back open.

POSTAPOCALYPTIC HEARTBEAT

I.

Drugged, I dreamed you a plume of ash,
great rush of wrecked air
through the towns of my stupor.

And when the ocean in your blood went toxic, I thought fire
was what we needed: serrated light through the skin, grenade
in the chest—pulled linchpin.

I saw us breathing on the other side of *after*.

But a blackout is not night; orange-bottled dreams are not sleep.

II.

I was a cross-legged boy
in the third lifetime,

empire of blocks in my lap while you walked
through the door of your silence,
hunting knife in one hand, flask in the other.

I waited for you until I forgot to breathe,
my want turning me colors only tongues of amaryllis could answer for.

It owned me, that hunger,
tendriled its way into my name for you.

III.

In a city made of rain
each door, a silence; each lock,
a mouth,

I walked daily through the spit-slick streets, harbingers on my hands
    in henna:

there will be no after

Black-and-blue-garbed strangers, they called me Cassandra.
(I had such a body then.) Umbrellas in hand, they listened
while they unlistened.

there will be no after   no.

the world will end   no.

you are the reason it ends   no.

you   no.

IV.

I didn't exactly mean to survive myself.

Half this life I've spent falling out of fourth-story windows.
Pigeons for hair, wind for feet. Sometimes I sing

"Stormy Weather" on the way down. Today, "Strange Fruit."

Each time, strangers find me
drawing my own chalk outline on the sidewalk, cursing
with a mouth full of iron,

furious at my pulse.

V.

After ruin,

after shards of glass like misplaced stars,
after dredge,

after the black bite of frost: you are the after,

you are the first hour in a life without clocks; the name of whatever
falls from the clouds now is you (it is not rain),

a song in a dead language, an unlit earth, a coast broken—

how was I to know every word was your name?

5

HISTORY, ACCORDING TO BOY

1

Boy is not one of the Boys, but Boy is observant.

At the edge of the basketball court in the park, by the locker on the far, far end of the locker room, by the punch bowl at homecoming, by the punch bowl at prom, nothing gets past Boy.

If you cut open Boy's head, at least fifty notebooks would fall out, each full of what Boy has written down with his eyes.

The Boys throw their words like sharp stones, and Boy takes note. Other notes: *nipples pressed against sweat-slick t-shirts during games of catch, bulges in basketball shorts and sweatpants, hands that are not his hands slipping below the waists of the Girls during slow dances.*

2

Some of Boy's notes are dreams.

These notes are recorded on the undersides of Boy's eyelids. After tonight's homecoming dance, Boy dreams he has the body of a girl,

a song only he can hear.

A war burns at the edge of the map Boy lives on.

On clear days, Boy can see smoke rising in the distance like an old god. Boy makes note of battles the smoke reminds him of: *Gettysburg, Wounded Knee, Atlanta.*

The Boys enlist. The Boys start wearing boots and camouflage hunting clothes to school. In the hallways, they shoot each other with guns only they can see.

They die bright, fantastic deaths every chance they get.

In English, D (one of the Boys) sprays the classroom with pretend bullets. The Boys clutch their chests and fall this way and that way.

D doesn't think to shoot Boy.

Below his desk where no one can see, Boy presses his palm against a pretend bullet wound in his thigh to stop the bleeding.

Boy thinks D is going to be a beautiful dead soldier one day.

Boy lives in a house made of guns.

At night, Boy's father and mother sleep curled around each other like snakes. The pistols and rifles on the wall above their bed twinkle like dark stars whenever a car's headlights shine into the room's one window.

Boy knows these things because Boy cracks open their bedroom door and takes note of how they hold each other in their sleep.

Another note: *They sleep like they are rehearsing for a play about sleeping.*

5

Boy's father takes him to the shooting range every Saturday.

Boy enjoys these trips as much as Boy's father does. It is their one good thing.

Their very first visit, when Boy was twelve, Boy's father stood behind him, traced his arms along Boy's arms, and gave advice about how to hit the black paper body a few yards ahead.

Boy was so busy concentrating, he took only one note: *The black paper body shuddered, then offered up its throat.*

"Here," the body said.

Boy made a perfect shot. Boy's father called over the other fathers to look at the perfect little hole in the black paper body.

Boy made note of how many times his father looked at him and smiled. *Three.* The number of times the other fathers patted him on the back. *Five.*

Boy was so excited he did a little hop. Boy noted that his father's smile dimmed then, but only for a second.

Boy's father has had that black paper body hanging in the garage ever since.

6

In tonight's dream, Boy kneels on the floor while D sits in a metal chair.

A bare lightbulb shines above them like a lynched moon.

(Boy takes note of this.)

Boy's heart is a grenade in his chest. Boy rakes D's body with his eyes. D is all muscle and blood. D has on a dirty white shirt; faded jeans; and a black hood.

The lightbulb turns red and Boy's hand trembles as he reaches for the fly of D's jeans. He pulls the zipper down slowly and reaches in.

Under his black hood, D moans. Boy holds onto him a moment longer—*so much heat*, Boy notes. Instead of a dick, hard with blood, the long end of a rifle juts out of D's fly.

Boy opens his mouth, leans forward, and flicks his tongue along the barrel.

In gym, Boy and the Boys sit on the floor while the coach models how to make a free-throw shot. Boy stops taking notes on form long enough to look at K out of the corner of his eye.

K sits with his legs wide open. K is wearing loose soccer shorts and, under them, loose plaid boxer shorts.

From where Boy is sitting, Boy can see up K's shorts.

Scratch, scratch, goes the pen in Boy's head. *The size of K's thigh, the scar on the left side of K's thigh, the muscles flexing in K's thigh, the curly hairs that begin on K's inner thigh—*

K throws out a word like a stone. Boy yanks his eyes from K's thigh and looks up. K's eyes are as narrow as knife wounds.

"Fag," hisses K.

All of the Boys are staring at Boy.

Sometimes Boy writes stories inside his head. The story Boy writes while crying in the restroom stall is about a kingdom where, every year on the same day, boys fall from the sky like dead birds.

Boy's English class is reading *The Iliad*. When Patroclus is killed, the Boys and the Girls don't understand why Achilles goes mad with grief. The teacher talks about male friendship.

"Fags," hisses K under his breath.

"Fags," hiss the rest of the Boys in agreement.

Boy is in the middle of writing a note about Achilles holding Patroclus's cold body when a spitball hits his forehead. The Boys laugh. Boy doesn't look up from his notebook. Boy's eyes are stinging.

10

A second war, in addition to the first war, has started. No one calls them "wars" anymore, but no one has bothered to come up with a new name either.

Boy watches the evening news with his mother and father. The newscaster talks about the two wars without actually using the word *war*, then he moves on to a story about a man found dead this morning. The body was in the alleyway behind a gay bar. Baseball bats were used.

When the newscaster says that police found the word *queer* etched into the victim's forehead, Boy's father shifts in his seat and changes the channel. Boy's mother asks if everyone is ready for dinner.

Notes on names Boy gets called at school: *fairy, pansy, fudge packer, pillow biter, cock gobbler*.

Boy reads about the myth of Ganymede. One moment, Ganymede is just a beautiful boy standing on a hillside. The next, Zeus descends upon him in the form of an eagle and takes the boy to live among the gods. The book uses the word *abducts*.

Boy wonders who wouldn't want to be abducted.

Boy makes an online profile. He says he is nineteen even though he is sixteen. Boy logs into the chat room and clicks on the profiles of other users. Boy makes note of different ways to say hello.

Boy: Hi there.

CollegeBoy78: Sorry, not into black guys.

Boy: Hey. What's up?

TNJock24: Not my type.

Boy: What's up?

Hot4Mouth: [this user has blocked your profile]

Boy does an experiment. He finds the picture of a white boy with a similar height and build and uses it to create a new profile. Boy finds the profiles of the same users he tried chatting with before.

Boy: Hey.

CollegeBoy78: Hi. What are you into?

Boy: What's up?

TNJock24: Not much. Nice picture. What are you into?

Boy: Hi there.

Hot4Mouth: Hey, sexy.

1 4

One afternoon, Boy gets home from school and goes to his bedroom to jack off. When Boy opens his bedroom door, he sees the gay porn magazine he has kept hidden under the mattress laying open on the bed. Boy's father sits beside the magazine.

Boy notes that his father's eyes are as narrow as knife wounds now, just like *the Boys'*.

Boy is a deer caught in headlights, a deer that could kill everyone in the approaching sedan simply by not moving. Boy's father holds his gaze like a driver who refuses to swerve.

All of the sentences in Boy's mouth come out broken:

"It isn't—" Boy says.

"I—" Boy says.

"I swear I—" Boy says.

Boy's father rolls up the magazine into a baton and stands.

Boy opens his mouth to say "Father."

Boy's father's fist comes down like war itself.

When Boy comes to, he's on the floor. A pistol rests on the bed where the magazine had been.

15

In line in the cafeteria, at his favorite table in the library, on the last block before the block he lives on, the inside of Boy's head is one blank notebook page after another.

16

One night, while Boy's parents are asleep, Boy steals his father's car. The entire drive, Boy prays the car doesn't break down. Boy doesn't know how he would explain his dad's car breaking down in the gay part of town.

This is Boy's second trip to the Throckmorton Mining Company. It's not a mining company, of course, but a gay dance club. Inside, it looks like an abandoned shaft and is lit with fake candles. A dead canary lies in the cage by the entrance.

The canary is not real is Boy's first note in weeks.

Boy feels eyes on him the moment he steps into the black light.

Boy has on a white shirt. He likes what black light does to his black skin. Boy feels the eyes on his body turn into hands on his body and the hands on his body turn into bodies against his body.

Boy hardly talks all night. There is a tornado inside Boy's silence. *Hades is not hell*, Boy notes.

The Stranger is old enough to be Boy's father. He has the body of a soldier. The Stranger's shirt is unbuttoned to show off his six-pack. Boy feels the Stranger against him before he sees him.

When they dance, Boy looks up into the Stranger's face for a moment. The Stranger has an easy smile. Boy makes a note: *Learn how to smile like that.*

When one song bleeds into another, the Stranger takes Boy's hand and leads him into a restroom.

Hades is not hell, Boy thinks again, this time with a man inside his mouth.

17

All of the lights are on in the house made of guns when Boy eases his father's car back into the driveway. Boy does not rush. Boy makes note of the number of steps from the garage to the living room. *Fifteen.*

Boy walks into the living room and walks right up to his father. Boy wonders if his father can hear the tornado ripping up the notebooks in his head.

Boy looks for his mother for a second, only sees the bottom of her feet at the top of the steps, then holds out the car keys as if to drop them in his father's hand.

Boy's smile looks like it has been cut into his face.

Boy's father's fist comes down like a war no one bothers to call a war.

In the biology lab, in the bedroom he is not allowed to leave in the evenings, at the dinner table encased in silence, *scratch scratch scratch* go the furious pens inside Boy's head. *Scratch scratch scratch.*

A third war starts and it doesn't even make the news. The same night that war begins, Boy walks down the hallway, cracks open his parent's bedroom door, and steps inside. He has been hold-ing the pistol for so long it is warm in his hand.

Boy stands just like Boy's father has taught him. Boy raises the pistol and takes aim.

Seconds are years in the almost-dark.

Scratch scratch.

The dull heat of the gun.

The vague smile on Boy's sleeping mother's face.

The way Boy's father murmurs for a second, then snores.

Boy stands beside their bed until his legs begin to ache. Boy brings the pistol down for a moment.

Boy has a name.

Boy whispers it once in the almost-dark,
smiles briefly, then takes a step back.

6

LAST PORTRAIT AS BOY

It's not barking, but the sound of teeth
just shy of sinew, taut insides of my thighs.

I'm in the woods again.

Branches snip my clothes into feathers, each step farther
into my own silhouette. Or

is this the locked room of my body?

A grown man called *boy*
gone inside himself,

the circle of wolves blinking gold
just beyond the trees.

I am not a boy. I am not
your boy. I am not.

NOTES

"Don't Let the Sun Set on You" is a found poem inspired by a February 21, 2006, *Washington Post* article by Peter Carlson titled "When Signs Said 'Get Out.'"

"Cruel Body" takes its title from a description of Tom Buchanan in *The Great Gatsby*.

"He Thinks He Can Leave Me" borrows its first line from *Edinburgh*, by Alexander Chee.

"Blue Prelude" references the song as performed by Nina Simone.

ACKNOWLEDGMENTS

I owe so much to the insight and care of my editor Erika Stevens, Rigoberto Gonzalez, Tayari Jones, Cynthia Cruz, Patricia Smith, Bryan Borland, Tom Hunley, Anna Journey, David St. John, Jericho Brown, Syreeta McFadden, Angel Nafis, DeLana R. A. Dameron, Isaac Fitzgerald, Roxane Gay, Tom Healy, David Groff, William Johnson, Ellen Claycomb, Duval Bodden, Ryan Henneberry, and Sally Squibb. I wouldn't be here without these people, nor would these poems.

I'm also incredibly grateful for the support of Western Kentucky University, Rutgers University–Newark, the NYC LouderARTS project, Cave Canem, and Queer / Art / Mentorship.

I would also like to thank the editors of the following publications, in which many of these poems have appeared, sometimes in earlier forms and under different titles: *West Branch, Guernica, Best Gay Stories, Jubilat, Hayden's Ferry Review, Blackbird, Weave Magazine, Vinyl Poetry, Muzzle* magazine, *Ishaan Literary Review, Spillway, Connotation Press, Line Break, Esque* magazine, *Naugatuck River Review,* the *Rumpus,* and *Bloom Literary Journal.*

SAEED RECOMMENDS THESE BOOKS FROM COFFEE HOUSE PRESS

SHOULDA BEEN JIMI SAVANNAH
Patricia Smith

978-1-56689-218-6

"*Shoulda Been Jimi Savannah* is a stunning and transcendent work of art, despite, and perhaps because of, its pain. This book shines."
—Sapphire

ANGEL DE LA LUNA AND THE 5TH GLORIOUS MYSTERY
Evelina Galang

978-1-56689-333-6

"Evelina Galang is a masterful storyteller and through her brilliant voice and craft, Angel and her family become ours too." —Edwidge Danticat

HOLD IT 'TIL IT HURTS
T. Geronimo Johnson

978-1-56689-309-1

"Transcendent contemporary American literary fiction, a rich and passionate story rewarding enough to be read again." —*Kirkus Reviews*

COFFEE HOUSE PRESS

The mission of Coffee House Press is to publish exciting, vital, and enduring authors of our time; to delight and inspire readers; to contribute to the cultural life of our community; and to enrich our literary heritage. By building on the best traditions of publishing and the book arts, we produce books that celebrate imagination, innovation in the craft of writing, and the many authentic voices of the American experience.

Visit us at coffeehousepress.org.

FUNDER ACKNOWLEDGMENTS

Coffee House Press is an independent, nonprofit literary publisher. Our books are made possible through the generous support of grants and gifts from many foundations, corporate giving programs, state and federal support, and through donations from individuals who believe in the transformational power of literature. Coffee House Press receives major operating support from Amazon, the Bush Foundation, the McKnight Foundation, the National Endowment for the Arts—a federal agency, and from Target. This activity made possible by the voters of Minnesota through a Minnesota State Arts Board Operating Support grant, thanks to a legislative appropriation from the arts and cultural heritage fund, and a grant from the Wells Fargo Foundation Minnesota. Support for this title was received through special project support from the Jerome Foundation.

Coffee House also receives support from: several anonymous donors; Mr. and Mrs. Rand L. Alexander; Suzanne Allen; Elmer L. and Eleanor J. Andersen Foundation; Mary & David Anderson Family Foundation; Around Town Agency; Patricia Beithon; Bill Berkson; the E. Thomas Binger and Rebecca Rand Fund of the Minneapolis Foundation; the Patrick and Aimee Butler Family Foundation; the Buuck Family Foundation; Claire Casey; Jane Dalrymple-Hollo; Ruth Dayton; Dorsey & Whitney, LLP; Mary Ebert and Paul Stembler; Chris Fischbach and Katie Dublinski; Fredrikson & Byron, P.A.; Katharine Freeman; Sally French; Jocelyn Hale and Glenn Miller for the Rehael Fund of the Minneapolis Foundation; Roger Hale and Nor Hall for the Rehael Fund of the Minneapolis Foundation; Jeffrey Hom; Carl and Heidi Horsch; Kenneth Kahn; Alex and Ada Katz; Stephen and Isabel Keating;

the Kenneth Koch Literary Estate; Kathryn and Dean Koutsky; the Lenfestey Family Foundation; Sarah Lutman; Carol and Aaron Mack; George Mack; Leslie Larson Maheras; Gillian McCain; Mary McDermid; Sjur Midness and Briar Andresen; the Nash Foundation; Peter and Jennifer Nelson; Schwegman, Lundberg & Woessner, P.A.; Kiki Smith; Jeffrey Sugerman and Sarah Schultz; Nan Swid; Patricia Tilton; USBank; the Archie D. & Bertha H. Walker Foundation; Stu Wilson and Mel Barker; the Woessner Freeman Family Foundation; Margaret and Angus Wurtele; and many other generous individual donors.

To you and our many readers across the country, we send our thanks for your continuing support.

LITERATURE
is not the same thing as
PUBLISHING

A 2013 Pushcart Prize winner, Saeed Jones is the author of the chapbook *When the Only Light is Fire* (2011, Sibling Rivalry Press). His work has appeared in *Guernica, Ebony,* the *Rumpus, Hayden's Ferry Review,* and *West Branch,* among other publications. Jones received his MFA in creative writing at Rutgers University–Newark and is the recipient of fellowships from Cave Canem and Queer / Art / Mentorship. He works as the editor of *Buzzfeed LGBT* and lives in New York.